My name is Adrienne C. Plummer. I am a teacher and candle vendor, poet and I do Spokenword. I go by the name of Ennedigo on TikTok, where I have Spokenword and candle videos. I am a widow and mother of three grown children: Justice, Josiah, and Javanna Plummer. I call them "The 3 Js." We currently reside in Chicago, IL.

I attended Percy L. Julian H.S. (Chicago, IL), and while there, I was a member of the school newspaper, English Club, and Gospel Choir. When Vanessa Williams was crowned Ms. America, I wrote a poem when I was 18, entitled *The First Black Ms. America*, which was published. I received a B.A. in English/Communications in May 1990 from Fisk University (Nashville, TN). While attending this HBCU, I worked on the Fisk Forum, the school newspaper (I interviewed TSU SGA president Jeff Carr during their protest back in the '90s); I also worked on the Fisk Herald (school poetry club); and in 1990, during their Homecoming weekend, I was honored to be "Ms. Fisk Herald." I pledged Kappa Sweetheart while at Fisk. This is an Auxiliary organization basically little sisters to the Kappas. I wanted to pledge a sorority but didn't have the courage or finances. However, as a Kappa Sweetheart, I remember the joy I felt when my line crossed and all of us performed at a Step show. It was a sea of red and white. I remember getting Kappa Sweetheart paraphernalia.

After graduating from Fisk University, I attended Roosevelt University (Chicago, IL; August 1990–May 1993). While a student there, I entered a writing contest. I wrote an essay on "Literacy". From this essay, I won the honor of Rubluoff Fellow. At Roosevelt University, I majored in Secondary Education. During the summer of 1993, I did my Student Teaching at South Shore HS (Chicago, IL), and in December 1993, I became a certified English/Language Arts teacher.

I have taught with the Archdiocese of Chicago, the Ford Heights school district, St. Mark Academy, the Chicago Public Schools, and Charter Schools. I am currently a 3rd Grade ELA teacher at a CPS school on the south side of Chicago. I hope to stay there another 10 years then I will retire and devote my senior years to Spokenword, poetry books and making candles.

I want to dedicate this book to my mother, my father, my grandfather, my sister, my niece, and my three children.

Adrienne Plummer

The CHI Brown Girl

Austin Macauley Publishers
LONDON * CAMBRIDGE * NEW YORK * SHARJAH

Copyright © Adrienne Plummer 2025

All rights reserved. No part of this publication may be reproduced, distributed, or transmitted in any form or by any means, including photocopying, recording, or other electronic or mechanical methods, without the prior written permission of the publisher, except in the case of brief quotations embodied in critical reviews and certain other non-commercial uses permitted by copyright law. For permission requests, write to the publisher.

Any person who commits any unauthorized act in relation to this publication may be liable to criminal prosecution and civil claims for damages.

Ordering Information
Quantity sales: Special discounts are available on quantity purchases by corporations, associations, and others. For details, contact the publisher at the address below.

Publisher's Cataloging-in-Publication data
Plummer, Adrienne
The CHI Brown Girl

ISBN 9798886938036 (Paperback)
ISBN 9798886938043 (ePub e-book)

Library of Congress Control Number: 2023923216

www.austinmacauley.com/us

First Published 2025
Austin Macauley Publishers LLC
40 Wall Street, 33rd Floor, Suite 3302
New York, NY 10005
USA

mail-usa@austinmacauley.com
+1 (646) 5125767

I want to thank God for being the center of my life. Through him all things are possible.

I want to acknowledge my stepfather for driving me to and from Chemo and bringing me snacks. I want to thank my sister and her family for picking me up after my 2 surgeries and my niece for drawing me the get well pictures. I want to thank my sister's friends Monica Broadie and her sister Anita Broadie for Edible arrangement after my first surgery, and my sister's two friends, Yvette Abrams and Ericka Bracey who gave me a certificate and a Brave Chic t-shirt during my cancer-free journey. I want to say thank you to "My Pink Butterfly," team who accompany me at Making Strides Breast cancer walk – my sister, her daughter, and my three children. I want to say thank you to my mother, Stepfather, and sister for supporting me and my three children in our times of struggle.

I want to say thank you to my Breast cancer team at University of IL hospital, and the plastic surgeon who performed my reconstructive surgery at University of Chicago hospital. (He has since gone on to a hospital in Washington, D.C.) I know I was just another patient but you helped me through my cancer journey with kindness, respect and laughter. Thank you for making me feel special during a very scary time. And thank you for the owner of Yehia and the stylist who helped me when my hair fell out after my first bout with Chemo. I paid $5 for a shampoo and I sat under a dryer for 5 minutes cause my hair had fallen out. (That was my first time having barely any hair) "It's only hair," the stylist said, "it will grow back." He told me this as I sat teary eyed.

I want to also thank any friends, coworkers, bosses who have encouraged me along the way, your words kept me going. I saw a post on social media the other day that read, "There is a blessing in the struggle." This blew me away. How profound this statement is. God puts you through test and it is in the struggle that you find your blessing. When you get through it you realize he doesn't give you more than you can handle.

I want to acknowledge any names of Basketball players, rappers, singer, movie- you are truly gifted in your craft. I respect what you do. Our lives are truly better now that you have shared your gift.

I want to acknowledge my hometown Chicago, IL. For all the great events, the Skyline, The Mag Mile, public transportation, politics, churches, our great mayors past and present and our former President Barrack Obama, First Lady Michelle Obama, and their daughters. This is a great city despite the bad rep it has gotten. It is an urban setting and with that said there have been struggles, conflicts, violence but the people of Chicago are truly great, the food is good and we have so many great Sport teams. One Love, Fam.

In Loving Memory:
Yolanda Howell
January 12, 1946- October 19, 2024
"Cake Lady" " Mommie" "Grandmere"
"You are the wind beneath our feet 👣"

The Chi Brown Girl

Brown girl from the CHI,
sometimes she's shy.
When you walk past her,
she might not say 'Hi'.
But on some days, she will,
it depends on her mood,
how she feels.
Usually, she's happy,
giving you a smile,
cracking jokes to keep you laughing.
Other days, she's quiet,
lost in thought,
thinking about Black equality,
women's issues,
social justice – it's a lot. 'Why worry?' you say, it's just the way she's made.
As a Black woman, mother of three,
She's striving to be
what God intends her to be, you feel me?
When she sees something not right,
she just might
engage in a fight
with words that ring true,
to give just due.
Her words are not meant to offend,
she intends
to bring about resolution,
so we, as American people, can mend.
There's going to be a shift,
uplifting Black people is the gift.
Just due,
for their labor, toils, tears,
and lives.
So Black people in the CHI,

Let's be peaceful and nice to each other,
setting an example other races can sample. Black love, Black pride,
let's embrace the new '60s with stride.
Like dominoes, it will pay it forward,
in God we trust, moving toward
a better future.

Crown

My Grandmother and mother used a pressing comb
To straighten our hair and make it longer
My hair was hard to grow
TLC don't you know
Shampoo, hooded dryer
These two never worked harder
Electric comb therapy
It was the remedy
To stimulate my scalp
My Grandmother had the skills
Knowledge of hair wealth
In 8th Grade I wore a Page Boy
With bangs
It bought my teacher so much joy
For my hair had grown
A sweet, shy young lady
She had known
With contacts and braces
Who could now make pretty faces
As a teenager in Highschool
I wore a Jheri Curl
It was so cool
It looked like a curly Afro
When I graduated
I wore it straight though
Wore my cap and gown
Our school colors were orange and brown
In college I wore a perm
I can still feel the burn
After college I wore it
In microbraids
Sitting in a chair for 8 hours
Easy to maintain even in a shower

In the '90s I ditched the creme
With a weave
I was Black Barbie reigning supreme
In 2014 when I went through
Chemotherapy
My stylist cared for me
My hair fell out
But he grew my hair back carefully
Then my hair was blond
He waved a magic wand
Thus I began my journey
Blond to red, the tides were turning
For a minute I have rocked my real hair
Red in color, nothing compares
Red Afro
Or red straight
Every hairstyle is trendy
And not late
Weave, wig or braids
Digging my African Hairitage
This is the way I am made

You Are Beautiful

Young Black child
Running free, running wild
Give your Grandma a smile
She knows after awhile
You will grow up
So much to show ya
So little time
Cause you will have grown up so fast
Your childhood won't last
Know that your Black skin
Is a prize you see
It was given by God
And it's free
Know that no matter
The shade of brown you are
You are a precious star
No need to change
You don't need to do a thang
Grow to love your hair
Whether kinky, curly or wavy
Don't let others who are shady
Make fun of God's gift
Their words should shift
To embrace difference
Black babies appreciate
Ignore the banter and hate
For your skin is one of a kind
It has melanin in great supply
Now hold your head in pride
Taking everything in stride
And you will be all right

Chicago

It's my kind of town
Chicago is
Winters so cold
A sheet of snow-blitz!
Better wear your big coat-shoot
Make that some more
Like hat, gloves, scarf, boots
And long Johns too
The commute to work is sometimes hopeless
Listen to your car radio-laughter relieves the stress
Mornings with Stevey Harvey
On V103
Sip your coffee or tea
Oh, no, you made a mess
Spilled liquid on your new dress
Now it's time to go
Move in the bumper-to-bumper flow
Soon as you go
Time to brake
Tomorrow you'll take the "L" for heaven's sake
Give your nerves a break
The "L" on the Dan Ryan is a faster commute
But you gotta watch so Brotha Man don't steal your loot
You got the Homeless, panhandlers, boys selling "Loud"
Oh, watch out for the lady, stroller and baby and another child
You have pastors preaching
And a young woman screeching
About what she is going to do
No, that conversation doesn't involve you.
Then there is the summertime
Yes, Summertime CHI
Is always so fly
There are so many festivals

Food truck fest
Taste of Chicago
Bantu Fest
African Fest – to name a few
Visit the Willis tower for a panoramic view
Ride in a boat on Navy Pier
Watch the planes in the air
At the Air and Water show
Visit the museums to remain in the know
We have
The Art Institute
The Field Museum
The Museum of Science and Industry too
Just so you know our downtown is called "The LOOP"
We have baseball cross town rivalries
Between
Chicago Cubs and the White Sox
We have Chicago Fire (our soccer team)
Our Basketball teams
Chicago Sky
Chicago Bulls
They wear jerseys and long shorts so supreme
We have the Black Hawks bring us hockey
And Chicago Bears football players so strong and cocky
Let's not forget
Chicago politics
Chicago voters don't like dirty tricks
Will vote you in, then vote you out quick
Better keep them happy
Never was a moment more sweet and sappy
When Obama bought Chicago a win
He was the first Black President
It was late after dark
When he and his family came to Grant Park
So many cheering fans
That were in the stands

Chanting, "Yes We Can."
With only a glance
The fans knew Obama had that hometown "charm"
He learned it from our late "Mayor Harold Washington."

BBall: Hoop Dreams

I really love watching Basketball
Jordan era says it all
Can I say 3 peats
MJ used to sweep
he played a mean ball in these Chi-town streets
the red and black team colors
Nike swoop Air Jordans
Chi-town can claim
Jordan's '90s reign
Now BBall has players like LeBron James
Stephen Curry and Kobe who have impacted the game
Each has won several rings
Shout out to Coach Jackson
Who won championships
With the Chicago Bulls and the LA Lakers
Loved to see their jerseys, long shorts
And cool sneakers
Oh, how we love
Our kicks
Collectors have players shoes
Others just have kicks with labels-so cool
The game of B-Ball is like Magic,
Karriem, Larry Bird, Dennis Rodman
So many good players
They are so tall and cool
Players like LeBron
Give back to the community
B-Ball way to pursue his dream
And make people happy
Building a school
In his old hood-very cool
Produced a show called "Buyers Remorse"
Also does "Taco Tuesday," with his daughter yo

My son has played B-Ball too
At the Y and in high school
Now working out-in the gym he stays
Steady playin' B-Ball these days
Once bitten by the B-Ball bug you never lose it
My son has Nike kicks and MJ hoodies

Crandaddy

I called my grandfather
Cranddaddy-
Cause my first cousin
Stevie
Mistook the G for a C
When he was little
He told me,
"That's Cranddaddy"
Cranddaddy was tall,
Light brown with wavy hair.
European features,
He could pass
I always remembered him in suits,
With a vest
Cufflinks
And a nice watch.
He worked at the Post office
-in Customs.
He was always well-dressed,
Always well-spoken
I never heard him raise his voice,
Or curse.
My mother was his twin.
I love her pics
On her Wedding Day,
It was of them two,
She in a white wedding dress
He in a suit-
She was straightening his bow tie.
His smiled in pride
As a tiny Tot,
Me, my mom and dad
Lived in Maywood.

Then when my mom
Was pregnant with my
little sister-we moved.
To Chicago-on 104th and Green.
3-bedroom brick house on the corner
We always had to rake
some many leaves
It had an upstairs attic apartment
And unfinished basement.
Before she went to work
Our mother dropped us off
At our Grandparents house.
We went to the Catholic school
Across the alley from their house.
memories during the summer
Getting ice cream from
The ice cream truck,
That came on their block.
We sat on the front porch to eat it
My 4 cousins, Cranddaddy, me, my sister.
I had vanilla-
They liked Chocolate.
I loved the rich, sweet taste so mellow.
Cranddaddy also showed us
A "Rootbeer Float"
scoop of Vanilla
And add root beer in a cup.
Other times he took us
To a candy store.
We would get a pickle
Bite it open and add a peppermint stick.
Sometimes we would get chips,
I always liked the cheese popcorn
And Barbecue chips-mixed.
I do recall
When my Sis and cousins

Would be playin' down the hall
I would sit in my Grandparent's room with
Cranddaddy watching Lawrence Welk.
It was a Talk show,
With Lawrence Welk as the host
Who would bring singers to the stage.
To this day I love a Talk show
and music is my rage.
Love the flow
Of a poem,
Or a song.
I would go on to watch American Bandstand,
Soul train too,
Would go on to join a choir
In school.
-and church.
Growing up I would sing
In the mirror
With tights on my head
First weave I guess.
In HS I bought LPs, 45s they were the best
Even had a Donnie and Marie stereo.
Play music high or low
So I guess you could say
Cranddaddy
Introduced me to music
Love of the beat ever since
My soul just loses it.

Sweet Sentiment

They say April showers
Bring May flowers
And in June
They are in full bloom
Hues of red, yellow, blue and green
Such a sight to behold
A majestic scene
Sunflowers are my favorite ones
Petals bright yellow like the sun
Flowers are special
On any occasion
Birthday,
Valentine's Day
Mother's Day
Prom and Graduation
When flowers are received
Tears of joy will be achieved
How can you resist the beautiful color
And fragrant scent
Pretty penny that was spent
Such a surprise
As you might surmise
Fills a heart with joy
Especially when given with
A new diamond toy
A ring,
A necklace
Or bracelet will do
Greatest way to say "I love you."

It's Time for the Youth to Make a Change

Sistas Who Led the Way

It's your time
we on our grind
so let's shine
blow their mind

Why hold back when they tryna throw shade
not good enough
self-esteem is in the grave
hold your head high
no need to be afraid
struggle was in the dues we paid
we are the right color
we are the right weight
as God gives us strength
we are now brave
the road ahead has been paved

Going the righteous way,
we will trailblaze
when we now speak
our thoughts will amaze
seeking true knowledge
ignorance replaced
we've been silenced
the truth is on display
playing homage to the Sistas that led the way
Queen Latifah
Lil' Kim
Lauryn Hill

MC Lyte
Salt & Pepper
YoYo
Mone Love
Missy Elliott
Left Eye
Foxy Brown
Eve

We Like to Dance

I can dance to the music
When the groove takes over
I can feel it
When my Sis and I were school age girls
Music was our world
We joined After school gym
Where we danced and twirled
We had tights and leotards
Our dance teacher was petite
And light
On her feet
We did a dance to "All Night Long," by Lionel Richie
Another dance by Prince called "Let's Go Crazy"
Our mother made our costumes
Checkered black and white dress was my favorite
On our block everyone was crazy about Michael Jackson
He danced so smooth, his steps were epic
My sister's friend taught a group of us a dance
To "Wanna Be Startin' something"
Our uncle told us not to play that song anymore
But we needed to get the steps just right
We also did a dance from MJ's video "Thriller."
Every kid on the block stayed up to watch this shriller
This video was about dancing zombies
At our Block Party we were like those dancing zombies
Each of us moving in time we never missed a beat
Doing a dance is all about team work
And a great dance teacher who gives that dream talk
Our hard work, extra practices, really paid off
The applause from all the neighbors said it all

Girl Friday

She was not just a
Pretty face
She had style
She had grace
Coming to work
Day in, Day out
She couldn't be replaced
Whether it was the coffee
And tea run
She could plan it all
Under the sun
From the meetings,
To the Pot lucks
To taking calls
To receiving the new copier
It always brought good luck
And lunch catered from the new "Food truck"
Water the plants
Spruce up the office
Typing a memo
To know when Boss
Needed a break
To giving advice
When it was needed
Even a pep talk
When the company
Had not succeeded
To letting the boss
Know who to hire
Who could motivate
And push the office higher
The Day in, Day out
Had become years

And now as she held
Her tears
Her boss was retiring
In June
He said it had not
Come at a moment too soon
He and his wife
Would move to a sunny shore
Travel the world and explore
What would become of
His Girl Friday
He brought her in
On a board meeting
Told her to have a seat and
Welcome her to the board
As a new member
He recalled she got
A degree last December
She had always been
An asset
Now it was her turn
To get an assistant
Train a young replacement
In her new role
She would make decisions
Tears streamed now
At this vision
Keep moving the company
Forward was her mission

Cooking

What I love about cooking
Is the aroma and taste
I am no longer a rookie
Certain seasoning can't be replaced
Spaghetti, fried chicken, pasta salad, tacos
Kale salad, Lasagna
Watch out that's hot though
So much fun to shop
For meals that I'm making
Grocery cart is filled with a lot
Here's a piece of fruit
Go ahead take it
Been cooking since
I was an 11-year-old girl
Food ruled my world
Still learning new techniques
Watching cooking network to learn new tricks
My family cooks too
We have a passion for good food
Sending each other pix
Of dishes we made
Giving each other recipes
Perhaps you can relate
Oldest daughter a baker
Son makes Jambalaya so mean
Youngest daughter seafood boil supreme
Each dish so delicious
Taste is so scrumptious
Going to a restaurant, or event,
Party or travel
We look for good food to eat and marvel
We love food with good quality
We are Foodies you see

Holidays are fun
We never cook alone
All four of us create a dish to share
Its family fun to be clear
Cheers

Juneteenth

Jesse Jackson said,
"Down with Dope,
Up with Hope."
James Brown said,
"Say it loud,"
"I'm Black
And I'm Proud."
King said,
"I Have a Dream."
Height of the '60s extreme
Little black, brown,
Red, yellow, and white
Children will hold
Hands.
Obama continued with
"Yes we can."
John Lewis said,
"Let's fight the good fight."
Fight injustice
With all your might.
Sojourner Truth said,
"Let My People Go."
Injustice no mo'
Harriet Tubman led the
'Underground Railroad.'
Blacks going up north
To ease Jim Crow heavy load.
Malcolm X said,
"By any means necessary."
Truly peaceful on the contrary.
Elijah Muhammad wanted
Black Economics
Black Business

Black Vendors
We don't need a piece of
The American pie.
Listen closely
I will tell you why
Black people
Are intelligent, creative
And also innovative
Making something
Out of nothing
Always has been our thing
Put our coins together-cha-ching
We are already wealthy
Putting Black dollars together is healthy
For our Black economy
As we celebrate this National Holiday
Let's remember our ancestors
Who served to pave the way
For Black businesses who now make the pay

Our Youth

I want to say Hooray
For all the Black Daddies
Who stand up for their children
They provide, educate, and mold them
They respect the Black Queen
Who carried their baby
They didn't hesitate or say maybe
Mama's baby
Pappy's maybe
True Black fathers proudly stand up
For their children when they are little
This goes a long way
For a young mind
For their will be a time
When the young one has their own
And they will remember the lessons
That they have grown and known
And even if the DAD is not in the child's life
Another Black man can raise a child
For it takes a village to raise a child
Whether they are mild
Or wild
It is worthwhile
For the entire Black community to raise a child
Let's get back to our African roots
Where the elderly would school the youth
It is tough now-a-days
Cause we have
Social media, video games
So much nonsense on the news
They give you the blues
Seems like the elders have given up on the youth
It's understandable some are disrespectful and rude

We can't reach them all
But the ones we do
Will go far in life,
They will carry the torch
I am so proud when I see youth
Who pay tribute
To their elders
Giving just "due"
For them they will be blessed
You have passed the test
Putting God first
And forget about the rest

Shoes

Some shoes for women
are not meant for walking
Wearing the latest heels
Your feet sore and hurting
Trying to look cute or
Look professional
You still look cute
In your kicks
In fact you look sensational
Whether you are working out
Or commuting to work
Your feet will shout
"I'm so happy."
In your kicks or low sandals
You could walk fast,
run for the bus
And run from trouble
Trust
And believe
You can achieve
Great things
When your feet aren't hurting
Men designed heels
To make women look sexy
I for one wear heels
Special occasion
I wear them for the pix
Then I am changing
Into comfortable kicks
Latest label
You can't say I don't look sick
With my beautiful kicks
Colors match my outfit

I know I am the "ish"
I use a foot spa
Lather my feet with
Crème's and lotions
Pedicure so tight
Colors are potent
Vibrant hues
Any color is my favorite
I take care of my feet
And they are pleased

Pretty Lady

Strong and independent
she makes her money
so she spent it
how she chooses
men are always friendly
want her to hold their arm
be his eye candy
wear that pretty dress
And stilettos
Be very classy
never act ghetto
but Mama didn't
raise a fool
she has knowledge
she went to school
she knew a degree
would come in handy
with prayer and hard work
she could live fancy
motto she lived by
do what you have to do
so you can do what you want to do
sometimes this mean
you do it yourself
don't ask for anyone's help
you work, save and invest
Let God take care of the rest
No strings-you don't need to stress
from a man who said I paid for that
when you pay for it yourself
you feel so accomplished
from the fruits of your labor
treating yourself you will savor

if a nice Gent comes along
she might slip him the
numbers to her phone
It is her hope they take it slow
do a Love Jones
cause even though she is independent
she does not want to spend her days alone
Maybe they can become a team
this is her ultimate dream

Positive Vibe

When you look in the mirror
Do you like what you see
Do you see a vision so lovely
Skin so smooth,
your crown full and healthy
Smile so sweet
You put on your favorite dress
It fits your frame
For you bought the right size
That compliments your frame
Make up done just so
Nails polished too
Grabbing your keys
You put on your shoes
Everywhere you go
People take notice
They see a confident woman
Who loves the skin she is in
As you smile and say hello
To everyone on your way
They greet you with a bright
Have a nice day
It boosts your spirit
It makes you feel nice
To know your inner voice
Gives you the spice

Lady Enne

No longer am I afraid
No longer will I keep quiet
I won't shut the fudge up
Your kindness won't buy my silence
I am fully grown
And I want to be heard
Did it ever occur
That I am more than just a pretty face
Or any other girl
As men like to replace
God gave me a gift
Which I plan to share
Letting go of self-doubt
Negative comments
And leering stares
I will not be objectified
To satisfy a whim,
A bet,
Truth or dare
Better beware
I am fully grown
Intelligent you know
Peace of mind each day grows
Soon people will see
God has prepared me
To bask in the light
To get a second glance
As I take my stance
For the unheard
For the pain
For the shame
I will adjust my crown
Replace my frown

With a smile
Cause I know
Trouble don't last always
Preservation
Determination
Courage
Always wins
In the end

America

History was not so great
Made some strides
Some laws fall back of late
How do we communicate
We are all part of the human race
"Injustice anywhere
Is an injustice everywhere,"
Dr. King said.
You know he was right
So let's right the wrongs
Broken people, broken homes
Find common ground
And before long
Our nation will set the tone
Justice here
Is justice there
Soon it's justice everywhere

Kicking Breast Cancer's Butt

May, 2015 breast cancer diagnosis
June, 2015 surgery
No choice in it
Right breast removed
Tumor removed
Body will be improved
September, 2015 surgery again
Test from June proved
Cancer had moved
To the lymph nodes
Some were removed
For my Boobs I wore a padded bra
October through December, 2015
Chemo monthly with the Breast cancer team
After the first time, I lost my hair
Feeling sad in a salon chair
Chemo was on a Friday
Being hooked to an IV for an hour
Watching TV and snacks I would devour
Time went fast
Happy when the final drip
Of the 2nd bag had passed
The day before my oldest daughter's college graduation
I had my own last day of chemo celebration
At my mother's house we live-streamed the ceremony
My daughter had finished in 3 years-her testimony
In February, 2016
I had radiation
5 days a week
For 5 weeks
Radiation made cancer weak
On the last day of radiation
I rang a bell

Radiation team gave me an autographed certificate
And wished me well
In October, 2016
I had reconstructive surgery
Fat from my tummy
Would create a new right breast
An 8-hour surgery-I would get hardly any rest
Every couple hour, I was given
Pain pills and a Heparin shot
It felt like a bee sting
The next day I was walking down the hospital wing
A 3 day stay in the hospital
I was ready to go home
To watch my favorite shows
Every October since then
My team "Pink Butterfly" comes alive
For the event "Making Strides."
It's a family event
Time well spent
I want to thank my family for their support
Because of you all, I never came up short

Kindred Spirits

Love is a complicated thing
It happens when you least expect it
It can give you great joy
Or make you emotional
And other times you can be blue
But don't give up on love
Even if you have lost
Rejoice in the memories
They were so worth the cost
I am a hopeless romantic
And I have romantic notions of love
Sometimes it is not returned
Cause the guy was in lust
whatever it is
don't give up hope
For you may meet the-One-and elope
You may meet at a place you go everyday
You could think you two are friends
You always talk-you have so much to say
Sharing intimate details of your life
You share with ease
So innocent at first
But lines get crossed-you joke and tease
Always wanting to please
Keeping up an image
Of being cool in their eyes
When they glance your way
your heart begins to race
Being shy you try not to leave a trace
But you wake each day
In anticipation
Of a look
A laugh

A conversation
Anything
Just as long as it's them
They make the mundane
So exciting
They are so entertaining
There is no need for explaining
You are already understood
It's the knowledge of before you could say
In a sentence he demonstrates
Such wisdom that leaves you speechless
Hanging on to every word is your weakness
Can this be real?
How is it he knows exactly how I feel?
How is it he feels the same deal
But he is a man
And I am a woman
Why does his words sound like mine
Hold up let me rewind
Maybe I will catch it this time
I said
He said
We said
To hear his words is enough
To shatter this exterior that is so "tough"
The road to get here may have been rough
But it is good to know I am enough
Blessing from God I raise my glass
Finally finding love at last

Way Life Goes

Sometimes it's best to be friends
From a distance
Don't need to talk on the phone
For instance
No need to share
The latest gossip
Or talk about
Your latest outfit
No need to take
Trips to the store
Don't need the
Company anymore
Not wishing you
Any harm
So don't be alarmed
I passed God's test
Of moving on without commotion
Having my peace is now my notion
And I am wishing you all the best
Take care and be blessed

Cherish Today

When I was eleven,
And my sister was seven,
Our parents got divorced,
It was 1976.
Our father moved to Seattle,
He had no choice,
Losing his family,
He couldn't handle it.
Summer of '76,
Our father we would visit,
Mom made the trip with us,
Then she left,
our father she trusted,
Would take good care of us.
That 2 weeks were
So much fun,
We did everything under the sun.
We ate Gumbo for the very first time,
Me and our father rode a horse,
But not my little sis, she was chicken, of course.
We climbed Mt. Rainer,
There was snow and ice up there.
We visited the Space Needle,
In a pond, we skipped pennies-what a ripple.
I drank tea so divine,
And we collected seashells each time.
We went to the beach,
My father would teach,
Us how to write him a letter,
He said letters and pictures would make him feel better.
Our mother called our father with some sad news,
She said our grandfather had passed,
Now I had the blues,

For he was my favorite person.
I wanted to go to his funeral,
To see him one last time in a hearse,
But our parents felt it best,
That we stay in Seattle to enjoy the rest
Of our vacation,
To be happy to see our dad,
But sad cause our granddad had passed.
How does a seven and eleven
Year old cope?
Life happens so fast,
Only memories last.
Cherish your time with your loved ones,
For tomorrow is not promised to anyone.

Jellybean

One Halloween
Our mother made us a costume so mean
Underneath it we wore our black leotard and tights
Then she had sewn a plastic bag dress drawstring
around the neck-so right
Inside the bag she placed colorful balloons
We were bags of Jelly Beans
Idea from a magazine-Boom!
We went to a
Halloween party on the block
All the kids were in shock
Costume so different and unique
Nothing bloody or ghoulish,
just something unique
That wouldn't make you shriek.

Becoming A Mother

Becoming a mother was scary at first.
Nothing prepares you –
You can't rehearse.
For 9 months, your belly had grown,
Then one day, your baby is born.
For me, I experienced the birth at home.
My water had broken that morn'
A phone call to my mom
Let her know it was time.
She left work, drove the distance
On I-290 to the Dan Ryan.
While I waited for her to come,
Contractions made it hard to lay down,
So I squatted,
My body – it parted
To bring forth a tiny life.
I cut the umbilical cord,
Then comes the afterbirth – oh Lord!
I tried to clean up.
Just then, my mother came home.
I told her my baby had been born
She was in a towel
On my bed in my room
My mom raced to get her,
My uncle, mom, daughter, and I in a car,
Drove to the hospital,
Which was 30 minutes – far.
My uncle dropped us off,
And we raced to the nurse's station with a huff.
When my mom told them what was up
They rushed me into a wheelchair and whisked me away,
Taking my daughter to a nursery, such a hectic day
I got a Demerol shot,

And then I was sleepy.
The next day,
They brought me my baby.
Oh my goodness,
She was a tiny lady
How do I feed, bathe,
And change her?
I would marry her father,
And we would have two more
Little ones.
My husband would pass
When they were young.
My mom and sis would help so that I wasn't alone.
Now they are all grown,
And I am so proud of each one.

Brown People

Our visit to San Juan, Puerto Rico
Was so much fun.
Each day, we went to the beach,
Laid on a towel in the sun.
We visited a museum,
Ate at restaurants,
And saw a walk of fame.
I fell in love with a drink
Called "Mango Mojito";
It was so flavorful,
With real juice and alcohol, yo!
It was amazing.
The native people
Were all so brown,
And we fit right in;
It felt like home.
We saw a sign:
"Black Lives Matter,"
And we were in awe
Every time we heard them chatter;
It was music to our ears.
We went to Walmart,
Dollar Tree, and CVS,
And we rode on the bus.
We stayed in an Airbnb
That was near an ice cream parlor,
But unfortunately, it was closed
Due to COVID.
We wore masks everywhere,
And we didn't dare
Go out after 9 PM,
Because of the curfew.
At the airport,

We had to show our COVID test results.
I hated that I had to leave so soon,
But I had to get back to work.
We vowed to come again,
And next time, we will stay in a hotel for sure,
Where we can ride in a shuttle bus
To get a tour of the city.
Love San Juan, Puerto Rico!

Lollapalooza

There is a summer concert in Chi Town
Called "Lollapalooza," where people get down
It has many stages set up
Where you get to choose who you want to see.
It's an exciting place to be,
With different artists performing
There is music playing all day long,
It's a 4 four-day event,
It is good money spent.
One year, me and my daughters went,
We had a blanket, no need for a chair,
Mainly standing in the grass –
Where people party their ass –
off.
I must say,
I enjoyed Childish Gambino the best,
He stood out from the rest.
He gave an outstanding performance,
His stage presence is enormous.
He can sing acapella,
His songs were so mellow.
He walked off the stage
And into the crowd,
Oh wow!
Getting up close and personal.
It was so cool,
When I saw his holograph on one stage
And him on another.
It was all the rage
The visual effects
Were so electric.
His song "Redbone" was my eclectic,
I put my hands in the air

And moved them with a wave.
The entire crowd swayed,
Grooved, and shouted,
They were truly stoked about it.
People took videos of his show on their phones
Post on social mediums,
With expediency.
So many memories, I see myself repeating them.

Road Trip

Whenever we take road trips,
We bring Pandora, maps, blankets,
Fried chicken, fruit, pop,
Bottled water, and chips.
One particular summer,
It was me, my son, and youngest daughter.
We were getting her stuff out of storage,
My son took the wheel first, he floored it.
I took the wheel second,
First time, no highway experience.
Scary at first, the appearance,
But once you get a groove,
You drive fast, you are on the move.
We rented an SUV,
(Best way to travel),
Stylish, roomy, and you get a good view,
Seeing the red dirt and mountains, we marveled.
Overnight stay at a hotel,
Up early next morning, we'll pack the truck,
And beat the rain with any luck.
Back on the highway,
In no time, we were flying,
Yet we ran into the rain anyway,
It was pouring, what a shame.
Had to pull over one time,
Then eased back in traffic, just fine,
Only to see down the road,
There was no rain at all,
But we had a ball.
Enjoying our tunes,
Eating snacks,
Fueling up and taking bathroom breaks every so often,

Road trips are the best,
As long as you plan and don't try to show off,
Because trust,
You can get lost in a heartbeat,
Stick to the flow of traffic on the main highway street.

Knowledge

You stare in amazement,
All that you did doesn't faze her.
Traps you set up,
She steadily dodges,
What is meant for her,
Is still on the horizon.
No matter what you do,
No matter what you say,
She still greets you,
She wishes you a nice day.
For you fail to realize,
She has knowledge,
It is plain to her eyes,
And knowledge is power.
Her kindness she will shower,
Listen to these words carefully,
Because she won't be missing her blessing.
You may be stressing,
And straining to see if she is failing,
But God moves all roadblocks,
So she is not fretting.
She won't be letting,
You take her joy,
So any ploy,
That you may have laid down,
God helps her manage to maneuver around.
So don't be surprised,
If she doesn't even try,
To get upset,
Or curse,
Or something worse.
For silence is the order,
She gives God all the glory.

MY 3J's
Co-written by Javanna Plummer

My 3 J's amaze me
When they were little, they'd drive each other crazy.
Welcome to Adrienne's world – toys galore.
They had everything from the store
From books to video games to ballet shoes and basketballs
My three little ones had it all.

They were troopers on their first plane ride
Seattle, Washington visiting Grandpa from their mom's side.
Visited the space needle
Ocean smells pungent
Trip from the past
They had a blast.
Mom and her sis
Took this same trip
Around the same age
Their first plane trip

We were big fans of HP
Wizards and goblins and make-believe
My oh my the unmentionable one.
They used to make potions for fun.
Hundreds of jelly beans – assorted ones.
Dressing in cloak feeling invisible
Three explorers, they were invincible.

First time in Chicago,
They went to a Magnet school.
My oldest made a Black book
She has vast knowledge of history
Good foods and she can cook

My middle child is computer savvy
Sporty, and he is married to ESPN
My youngest is a teacher, a journalist
Artsy clothes and make up
Set the trends.

In college, they were HBCU-bound
Following the path their mom and auntie set
Southern collegiates
Oldest finished in three years.
Middle child was a standout amongst his peers.
Youngest got two degrees and pledged Blue and white.
My proudest moment, we got it right.
It took a village to raise the tykes.

Great wisdom, activism
And a love of good cinema and television.
From the soundtrack to the script
And the character's wit.

Comedy, drama, or a romance flick,
We watch it all.
A close-knit family,
My 3 Js and me

Acceptance

Co-written by Javanna Plummer

"That's all she ever wanted, you see," she said.
"She was not light,
Skin was dark
To some, she was not pretty
But she was sharp
Witty
And smart…"

She was petite
Funny and sweet
Always a smile
From cheek to cheek

In 4th grade got my first library card
Read lots of books; read my book report aloud
I was proud to be a bookworm.
I lived for the applause when it was my turn.
Brown girl in a brown dress,
Bangs and a bun, grinning from ear to ear.
Sending school photo to father so dear.
An artist would recreate the pic.
I was so proud of it.
I had braces as a youth.
Silver, and metal were woven through each tooth.
No popcorn or taffy for me.
Always kept a toothbrush handy.

In high school, I joined the English club and reported school news.
I was a young Nancy Drew.
She was my introduction to detective stories,
Which became a key part of my allegory.

SVU and Monk on repeat.
In college, I developed a writing beat.
Poetry club and journalism
Led to an internship at a television station.
I interviewed the president of SGA.
I saw activism on display.
I wrote a poem about Miss Black America and her newfound crown.
I finally saw royalty in Brown.
Years later, I took an online class
I fractured my ankle and I wore a cast.
Wrote a story about an athlete who was always swift and fast.

While playing, he got hurt and had to wear a cast.
But only for a moment; hoop dreams always last.
They say in life, when one door closes, another door opens.
Before I knew it, I was saying words unspoken.
Soon, I'd perform in front of guests
After I got my start at a poetry fest.
Some days I felt so stressed, I became a WordPress
Until I wrote enough to fill a book.
Thirty poems was all it took.